Petals

Petals

Poems

Brian Thomas

Dedicated to my dear friend
Michael Dunn
Businessman, journalist, 1953-2020
Someone I could always rely on and who made me laugh

Maroon petals in an envelope
A hurried note and a kiss
Return of a picture of you
Drawn at a fete at Christmas
I can guess so easily:
You want to say
Goodbye

Poems

II Antagonism

III Resolution

IV Epilogue

x

Preface

Back in July 2020 I posted a couple of poems of mine on Facebook, the humorous *The Ivory Owls* and the more serious *Petals*. They were rather well received and several friends suggested I publish a book of them. So I decided to launch two collections, as the pieces chosen seemed a little incompatible in one volume: the comic *When Rabbits Go Bad* – a selection of poems, song lyrics and cartoons – and this volume, *Petals*, with more soulful stuff, kindly illustrated by Anon-D-Zyne, creator of the on-line *Petals* images sourced from one of my more spectacular roses.

Petals stretches from the present year back to the 1960s, stopping at various points in between to record incidents, thoughts, passions, friends, lovers, summers, winters, music and times both good and bad: all the things that make up a life. They contain observations that are, hopefully, not too naive for these challenging times.

There were specific periods when I wrote this kind of material and the moods of those times filter through to today. There are memories most cherished, as are many of the people who populate them either as leading lights or background characters. Some pieces are sad, some are sombre, some bright, some might even be dubbed wry; some have notes, most do not (and why would they?). However you rank them, I hope you enjoy these lines, in all their various forms, and spending a little time swimming through someone else's ocean of consequences.

Brian Thomas, Winter 2020.

I Beginnings

The Wall... When I Was a Child

The wall never came down to the edge of the river
When I was a child.
It merely stood, a bricked and mossy bastion
As dividing line between two groups of lives
Number three and number five
(and number seven on the leeward side).
Our garden was our ship, our battleground, our haven of rest
When I was a child.

Then the mechanical diggers came, and the mixers,
The blocklayers, bricklayers and carpenters, the noise
And the few nomadic birds that came to rest
On our brown and battered paint-peeled feeding table
Did not call quite so often.

There were chickens in the homely coop on the wall side
That long and lumbering wall with craters for 'gators
And lots of hidden things
From out of which stories are formed
Behind the secretive green of the mosses and ferns.
My dear grandmamma loved those comb-like leaves.
The chickens died, eventually
(Of old age as no-one had the heart
to sacrifice them for a meal)
So did my grandmamma. Cancer.

1

When I was a child
There was nothing to do
But pedal-cycle up and down the cracked pavement
And swing from the little roped seat beneath our lincoln sycamore.
And I remember the aged Mr Hall and his lady wife
Shouting for us to move our metal donkeys
Away from their gate.
The donkeys left for other pastures
But not too far away...
Hee-haw, haw-haw.

And just along the road apiece
There was... Sally? The only Sally I ever knew then
The only Sally I ever loved.
Or was it... Was it that gleaming red tricycle
That first caught my gaze?
And the way her yellow hair used to curl and turn
Just like the emerald grass used to swirl
In the wind, on top of the wall.
Our wall
But that was so long ago
When I was a child.

Then the years passed
And the house, our tall, grey family box of seeds…
The seeds scattered: some died, some simply faded
And the old stairs creaked with the fall of padded feet
No more.
And the contractors finished their grand re-scaling
And who then could recognise what had been?
Only the wall,
Still and silent (but for the winds), remained
To look sadly on
(If indeed walls feel pain)
At what was and what Here had become.
Perhaps it might remember our games
(And the games of family children long before),
Our loves and losses
And all the words spoken,
Cries cried, shouts of joy and pain
Echoing against that remarkable wall
In an age lost
When I was a child.

Stragglers

Autumn at Gyllyngvase, Cornwall, 1960s

The stragglers are here again
Sitting on the beach.
It's as if they've been there all season
It's as if they had no reason to realise
That summer's slipped beneath their feet.
And yet, they linger
Wringing out the very last glimmer
From an aching sun.
Their deckchair props rattle
In the chilly September breeze.
A few are on their knees
Building sandcastles which rise,
Live a moment, then fall once more,
Often to the leading edge of a sizzling wave.

The lairy dairy ice cream man
Waits in the wings
For an occasional shilling
From a kiddie willing
An overcoated, bloated parent
To buy him a jolly lolly
Or a rub-a-dub tub.
A toddler tests the ocean's paddling promise
As guinea pig for a dubious mum.

No-one swims.
The rock-a-by-wave raft
Has been pulled up the sand to the road
Leaving deep indentations
To be filled by palpitations
From a spume-led tide.
The rocks look bleak,
Not sleek and meek
As they seemed in June
With enticing pools of ocean life
And lime green weed
Damp enough to make footfalls wary.
The sand is crimped with the prints
Of feet once visiting
The land of the never-known.

Back to Birmingham and Stoke
Why not poke your head in at Pontypool?
Can you not drag yourselves away?
There's always another year, you know.
Or are you reluctant
To let this one go?

The numbers dwindle.
Night is coming
And the flotsam
blots them
away…

Barbecue

*An episodic memory of a Sixties adventure on an isolated Cornish beach
with a murmuration of friends – flocking, foraging, finding fun.*

Barbecue

left the car lane-bound above the grey pebblebeach
scrambled down root-veined cliff face carrying bottles
like a wine waiter nervously negotiating a flight of steps
with both shoelaces undone
half the troop are already here, by a limp fire
smould'ring beneath the grating of its charcoal tray
Who's got the matches?
I have!
Let's have some more wood!

11

she kneels by the dumb fire
prodding it now and then
praying for the odd spark
knees pressed deep in the sand
legs folded beneath her
. blonde, smiling,
adjusting a red cravat at her neck
she says she plays guitar
but she did not bring it
What's the lard for?
Cooking!
curlyhaired chef in jeans
the face that launched
a thousand sausages
(thou sand)
(m)anna
Trampqueen
Hello.

Surrounded, alone
advancing sea and forest
tonight (we hope) at peace
Call out your name and see
Echoechoechoecho
silence
then crashing branches, somewhere
fire wood spinning down the cliff
driving missiles of deracinated rock
to join in convoy and excited chatterchip

13

a gathering of friends encircle the freshly-built bonfire
a ripe blaze itself walled by surf-smoothed stones
a miniature Stonehenge
and, not far behind, curly's barbecue
a headlong car dash for saucepan, fork and scissors
bearing fruit
Anyone want a half-cooked sausage?
no takers
yet.

climbing the cliff with her boyfriend
she looks back
The sea is calm and clear, he said,
That is a sign...
But he didn't say of what

my little transmutation of gold, here tonight
she stands on the water's edge with three friends
talking, distractedly engaged
occasionally she looks my way and smiles
I want to go and speak to her
but I cannot; it's not my place
the girls are grouped apart, the boys clustered telling blue jokes
to cross to her side is to cross the thin red line
between fact and fantasy, peace and ridicule
and I cannot
Jackie: golden, distant, joyful

night falls quickly
when you're having fun
too quickly
the log-laden fire glows orange at dusk
and waits to die
we had to move it
encroaching sea quenching threatened
and now the wavelets lap over Stonehenge
water hisses and steams like a mediaeval dragon
Adrian rescues the frying pan
taking over from our glamour chef
"Mole" (his sobriquet) is fishing
joker, angler (hiccup) has caught only one fish
small, nondescript, inedible
the fryer (his chum) keeps the party going
a human terrier, a Dandie Dinmont
in swimming trunks, skin flame-lit
blood-scored in silhouette:
a young Hiawatha
without feathers (suggesting hopelessness?)
inane comments, native American whoops
tosses the quiet girl in the green bikini a roll
she flicks back the nut-brown hair from her eyes
and eats
my goldengirl leaves
Mole packs up his fishing gear
(just as well, as we keep tripping over it)
starts to hover round a carrier bag of beer

the fire begins to expire
What games can we all play?
muttermutter... Murders?
How the *blank* do you play that?
Curly, ex-cook explains:
a "murderer" is picked
all run for the bushes
Oh, yea – and that's the last we see
of the intertwined couples
Should be great fun!
runrunrunrun for your lives
your friend might be a killer
cravats stand out in the half-light
especially red ones
I follow the red cross
for she cannot be the mur...
AAAAAAAAAAAAAAAAAA
a cry from across the beach
a victim! Hurry back
unfortunately... it's all over
forgotten
and the murderer? well...
another time perhaps
another beach barbecue
before the long and languid summer ends

making love by the fire to the crack of the twigs
drinking from a bottle of cider (*Pass it on!*)
vicar's daughter joins in rugby song choruses
What's black and comes out of the ground
at a hundred miles an hour?
A mole on a motorbike!
Hey! cries "Mole," breathing ale fumes over everyone

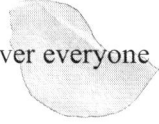

later
we make our way back
in the dark, up the cliff face
a smouldering heap of charcoal, our gift to the tide
perhaps someone else will rest by our fire tonight
(before it fizzles out of Now to Never)
and ponder who was here and why they came
and the pebbles are abandoned again (*Ooh, my feet!*)

ten white eyes illuminate the road
doors slam, night birds chatter
and suddenly it's OVER and we are leaving
and all that's left is a memory of what could have been
of a girl in a green jumper and royal locks
with a burning smile guaranteed to melt your heart
in a single sizzling twist
I wanted to walk with you
but your girlfriends' eyes warned interlopers
to keep their distance
and the beer is gone, "Mole" is drunk
burbling to himself in the back seat
and I am tired
the only failure was my own
but Life's strange encounters persist
tomorrow, see her
perhaps
(*Mind that damn great rock in the road*)
perhaps...

The Seagulls of St Ives

1

We flew down the hill with our hearts in our hands
To an autumn-smoke town that was sleeping
On a chill, dreary winter day blowing our hair away
Far from the fog that was weeping
And I looked into your eyes
Tried to find the measure of your love
That would illuminate all of your sighs
But there was nothing but the seagulls of St Ives.

2

We took refuge inside a hand-painted cafe
Where the food was for thought not for eating
And the colours that hung around clothing the walls and ground
Shattered the bowl of our speaking
And I held a kaleidoscope in my hand
And tried to make you see that I was really made to be
And not skilfully planned
Beneath the halo of the seagulls of St Ives.

3

We ran to the jetty and gave time a kick
Chose some suitable words for the occasion
Switched on to a meal which made us both feel
We were eating in some disused station
And the people across the room
Tried to read us with their eyes, tried to minimise our size
Tried to discord our tune
Destroy the singing of the seagulls of St Ives.

We sat for some time opposite one another
Your jet black seaside-sentimental hat
Tipped jauntily over one eye.
I was wearing a stripy, grey Edwardian jacket
With out-of-place plastic buttons and a black shirt.
You were all in black.
Which really said very little for the way we felt about it all.
And about the way in which the day
Had lengthened into an Indian summer.
And the fun-weary deckchair-dealers
Watched with sulky disapproval as we ate our fill.
A disapproval changing to surprise
On the production of a £5 note.
They watched us leave.
But not one face showed a different light from another.
As standardised as their tremulous currency
And as controlled
And jealous of the fact that we
Could never be controlled...

4

There was nothing to say, there was nowhere to go
For the sun and the trees set us dreaming
Of a world without fear, of a seasonless year
Of cities with animals teeming
As we lay down on the shore
Wishing thoughts across the sea to a future we could be
If we could settle the score
Repay the debt owed to the seagulls of St Ives.

27

On a Misty Morning, From a Clifftop

The small, grey, motored, mast-stabbed

Fishery-free lifeboat

Chalks a deliberate bow stream behind

And stretches its destiny

To the edge of the sky.

For a moment it veers landward

Then, as if changing its mind,

Turns sharply seaward.

The black-flap envelopes of ripples

Open and close in a whisper

And the mist of the morning

Drifts like a dream

Into the sun's embrace.

Paper Boat

Sail away, sail away
Little paper boat
And take my dreams with you
The emotions of my life
Now decorate your decks
And sails, in cursive ink
And take my love with you.

Take the easy stretch
And avoid the heavy currents of the waterfall
Travel to the sinking sun
Where the willow hangs alone
And take my heart with you.

Sail along through the weeds
Little paper boat
And do not pause to cry
For the message that you take
Of the summer that I knew
Must never see the sky.

Take the final turn
And disappear into a night's oblivion
As the pyre of Boromir
Spelt the ending of an era
Take my life with you.

From Sketches of a City – Winter, 1972

A massive stretch of land has been raised to the ground
by the city council in preparation for a major redevelopment.
The area is corralled behind a dilapidated, vandalised wooden fence
and overlooked by a huge billboard advertising a major airline.
In the centre of this expanse of rubble lies a small parish church,
perhaps a single island of defiance.

From Sketches of a City – Winter, 1972

The Island

I

The city council regrets
That God must go.
Besides,
you can get much nearer
to Him now
by jet airliner.

II

We felt safe on the island
until they closed the doors
and vandals broke the windows.
Even though our walls were scorched
with the black marks of wartime
we thought we could be
impregnable again.
But though bombs were avoided
and bulldozers rebuffed
we could not fight
our Pilate,
Progress…

III

St Stephens'
stained glass eyes
are already blind,
but there is no enemy advance.
Are they drawing lots
on which workman
shall remove
the first stone?

33

Misplaced

Where is this lonely, copper desert
That tortures my heartbroken eyes?
Why am I here?
Emissary of a land
Where trees are not
Spindly afterthoughts
Fighting their way
Up through the filth
And hills
Are not the discharged remains
Of excavators.
Only the children
Offer a smile
For they have never seen unfettered stars
Nor dreamed beyond the ends
Of their streets.

Postcard

Through a window veil of lace
I can hear the heavy bumbling of the traffic
See the traceries that elaborate your face
Hear the sighs of the strangled city.

A monster of a moon
Sneering silky cloud props,
Finger-spread, cardboard light:
A robed strobe, silhouetting your absence.

There is more to see and hear.

Turning a troubled eye to orange pavements of Autumn
Past the pac-a-mac bric-a-brac patterns
bedevilling the leaves
A dogbark breath invades the street
And moulds those irregular passers-by
Into a cloak of indifference:
Coats without faces,
Gloves without hands

And beyond this inch by inch reference
On a map carved deep across your skies
Lies Freedom
Air
Trees
And your love.

Thoughts

I
You are
That once and once only dream
Sparking my night
With sequins of your essence.
May the broken-faced alarm
Of "sanity"
Never rings.

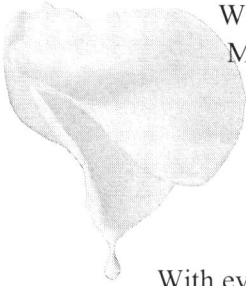

II
With every dance of the teatime curtains
My mind is drawn far into the void
And somewhere, in that lost place,
You are calling me
And I cannot
Find the words to reply.

III
Summer's epaulettes rest on the shoulders
Of a snowy season
Sun showers refresh the day
And snow banks hide the river
From the multitude of dreams
Cast like a shiver in the water
And home is a castle on a crag
Just out of reach…

Sciurus Vulgaris

Across the tarmac surface
Of the sparkly, rain-speared motorway
Heading home, at last
In a furry flash of gold-brown lightning
Splitting the cars in two
Dividing by borderline
Carving an invisible trench
At no time being aware of left or right
Only before and beyond:
A squirrel
On his journey between the seasons.

II Antagonism

Inn by the Water's Edge

Perched on stools you merry minstrels
Sing the night away with your songs
Which echo far out across the bay
Sing on, with soft accompaniment
From lapping February waves.

Sup your beer, yon bearded player
Wipe the froth from whiskered lips
And play on; your colleague at your side
Her skirt rides high and teases
Hair hangs long and low, untangled seaweed.

Cheers for more excites the gathering
Wait, replace a broken string
Wait awhile, another sip of beer
Then one more song vibrates the air
And people edge towards the bar.

Suddenly the tempo changes
Solo sad song, room goes quiet
She plays on, Gauloises smoke spirals
Glasses no longer chink, hands meet
Familiar ballad, hits the heartstrings
One hundred lips narrate the words.

Faces pressed in faces' tresses
Swaying to the gentle rhythm
Of the much-loved tender mantra
Bearded player, mute this time
Lights two cigarettes and smiles
One light for him, one light for her.

Perched on stools, you merry minstrels
Sing the night away with your songs
I thank you for a grand distraction
Sing on, sing on, for those who stay
For we have moved to outside darkness
Behind, the fire, the light, the kindness
And the echoed singing on.

Dead Eyes, For a Moment

I stepped over a pair of dead eyes
In a gutter puddle
Head down
On a dreary day.
They stared, startled
As if aware of a sudden new presence
Then eyed the interloper
With disdain.

I said nothing
And the eyes gave no sign.

A falling droplet from an awning
Kissed my neck,
Ran inside my collar
And, momentarily, the eyes wandered
Out through the eternal circle
Of that dreary day;
When they returned,
They had softened

I winked
And they winked back
And then I turned into the face
Of the slackening rain.

Eyes less dead, I set off once more
The day seemed brighter
I even summoned a small whistle.

47

Paper Chase Revisited

The game is simple:
Take a slice of chalk
And dust an arrow on to the ground.
Take the lead, lady
If you need to feed the fun
I cannot come.
A cluster of cars waiting
Anticipating in the evening air
And a handful of players
Who have been waiting
And waiting.
Waiting for the fun to begin
Disappointment mustn't show
Away you go!
And catch the leader
With her dusty fingers of chalk
And her giggling trail of arrows.
I remember doing it before
But then there were so many more
So many more…
Most of you – no, ALL of you
Can't remember back that far
Into the minute book.
There was Sue and Cherry,
And Derek and John,
Keith and Bobby,
David and Robert,
Vivian and Barbara,
Sandra, Peter, Helena…

The list, incomplete
Seems endless
As endless as those days once seemed.
But they are ended
For me, they are gone
And you cannot cover new ground
With old tricks.
Not for me.
The sun shone then, as now,
But its secret smile has gone.
Is my dream my future
Or is my dream merely my past
Trying to live now?

Do You Want to Know?

I think this covers both sides of the issue

We've knocked upon the door of your house
You're the first house in the block
Will you listen to the words we say
Before you snap the lock?
We've travelled in from Canada
To spread the word around
We're not book salesmen, may be leave
Some pamphlets to astound?

Do you want to know about love and peace?
Do you want to know about Jesus Christ?
Will you listen to our message
Or refuse to look at us twice?

We've called upon the old and sick
And children with the Word
They've looked at us quite blindly
Just as if they haven't heard
We've tried to pass our wisdom on
But they don't understand
We feel so lost and helpless
In this Godforsaken land.

We don't come selling jewellery
We don't come selling toys
We want to know what you believe
Have you made the right choice?

We'll call again next Thursday lunch hour
If you read our text
May we suggest page four of three?
There's no need to be vexed
We'll talk about direction
And the final road of Man
We'll pump our theories down your throat
Until you understand.

Do you want to know about love and peace?
Do you want to know about Jesus Christ?
Will you listen to our message
Or refuse to look at us twice?

Fever

I remember
sending you to sleep
with songs and poems
while your sudden fever
fought back
and scorched your brow
with summer sun fervour.
I remember
but I do not know why.
All in know is
you are gone now
and all I have
is the sad replay
of some of the songs
that made you well.

Folk Group, One November night

Two pretty girls singing their hearts out
Bright and young with red rose bouquets
Mini-skirts in black and red high heels
Clapping, laughing, spellbinding the crowd.

Two lead guitars, both playing rhythm
One lead guitar, lead-lines all thumbs
Singing songs we should be proud of
Prompting high cheers from everyone here.

Said they would play for part of the evening
Started at eight and sang long past ten
Paused at nine to sample some coffee
Playing requests then, right up to the end.

Two pretty girls packing equipment
Rhythm guitarists discussing a song
One lead guitarist depressed in a corner
Seems he was told what to do with his thumbs.

Magdalen Mine: January 12, 1974

Magdalen Mine: January 12, 1974

A gash in the rock
Eight of us to pierce
With a shaft of torch light.
Sliding on mud
Treading warily
Deep under the earth
In a giant's throat.
Listen, the echo
Of a falling stone
Invisibly skittering
As it falls
Hitting with a crash
Swallowed with a gulp
At the black centre of the icy shaft.

Lightning, photoflash!
Captured forever
Frozen in a lens
To grace an album.
The high ceiling leaks
The tears of miners
Long forgotten
They plop into leaves
Decorate her hair
Sink into his coat
A sad testament
To a sudden-felt fear
Without a name.
The air smells of a distant past
To others, merely of mould.

Outside: the winding, leafy path upwards
To the edge of an eye-socket crater
Encrusted with lichen – steep, inviting
Begging to be explored by the intrepid.

An empty tunnel
A hint of rockfall
A fragile spider's web
Desiccated, tremblingly lit
With water-droplet lights.
To photograph it
Is to destroy it
To look upon it
Appears irreverent.
There are no spiders now
And the walls are wet.
Huge wooden rafters
Creak, dribble water
Into our hands
Like an ancient,
Weeping saguaro.

The adits are blocked
At least those
That remain visible
The rest are lost.
A way of life has
Mysteriously, wretchedly
Vanished from the earth
(in every sense).
The tunnels speak
In a language defunct
With a tongue not geared
For the language of today.
I cannot believe
I try to respect
Yet cannot imagine
How it was, once
I can only dream.
Eight of us leave – awed.

Magdalen Mine: Notes

Many years ago, I discovered the history of the one-time Magdalen mine whilst researching material for features for the *Falmouth Packet* newspaper, when I was a fledgling reporter there. I popped out to the location with *Packet* photographer Peter Chesworth and he took a series of pictures of the overgrown site to accompany my article. We were both a little too well dressed to be thrashing through the bracken, but still, it was all in a good cause. That's me below, captured by Peter, gazing out with suitable photographic whimsy from the mouth of an old adit and looking back at the dangerous descent to get there – plus the mine as it was, a structure long gone on our seventies visit.

On the strength of this visit, I had a minor brainstorm and decided to escort a party of Young Conservatives down into what was then this highly dangerous stretch of sloping, overgrown scrubland, to see what remained of the old workings. Close to the railway viaduct at Ponsanooth, Cornwall, it's probably now a lethal place to go, with a further fifty years of abandonment approaching. Fortunately, no-one fell down any holes in the ground back in 1974 and nothing collapsed on our heads in this foolhardy venture, so we were pretty fortunate. I don't recall what my friends thought of the experience, but at least I was hoping to get some nice flashlight snaps of them peering into the gloom of an old cavern or thrashing through the underbrush. Unfortunately, the film jammed in the camera and those shots never materialised. Still, I recorded the moment in a poem – written before I discovered there were no snaps of the visit.

Magdalen Mine: The history and what followed

My seventies article began like this.

A little below Ponsanooth, on the south bank of the river, immediately adjacent to the railway viaduct, lies a long overgrown feature of the Cornish landscape. Beneath a spreading umbrella of woodland trees the hidden Magdalen Mine gradually rots away, in form and in local history.

Thick bushes and barbed wire fences bar the paths and block sleepy adits where once an industrious workforce laboured. Evergreens weep rainy tears into silent, yawning shafts once filled with the chink and rumble of mining activity.

Records for the mine go back to at least 1522, when payments for toll tin were noted from the then 'Mary Mawdlyn Myne in the Manor of Cosawes.' In 1730 there were some 17 shafts listed alongside open workings with a further seven to the east in Cosawes Wood. Whim Shaft, from which the tin was brought up, was 50 fathoms deep, others varied from 20 to 30 fathoms. A few years after this the site was abandoned and in 1805 the *Royal Cornwall Gazette* reported that several hounds, a hare and a deer had fallen into an open shaft some 104ft deep.

Fresh works were instigated in 1809 and in the following five years £2,000 was spent on a water wheel, a new leat and timbering for "the great adit." But money ran out and plant and machinery were sold off in 1820. It was revived between 1913 and 1921, producing about four tons of "black tin" every month; in its latter hayday it produced ore averaging up to 12lb to the ton. There was a further brief pause in operations and these resumed in 1926 but the mine finally closed down for good in 1930 when the market price for its product collapsed.

Nothing now remains of the once illustrious Magdalen Mine except the faint inroads in vegetation which mark the passing of carriage roads and the ever-present gaping holes, constant reminders of busy shafts. The area is carpeted with a profusion of bluebells, and punctuated with brambles – silent, beautiful, but for the careless visitor it could be dangerous.

Shortly after this piece appeared, I got a phone call from 85-year-old Joe Bartlett who said he was probably the last miner to have worked at Magdalen and had never forgotten his experiences over a ten year tenure. I drove out to his home near Helston and the subsequent interview made a second fascinating feature, along with a superb photograph of Joe (Peter on the lens again), which he treasured.

After the story appeared, I received an unforgettable letter from Joe, which I have kept ever since amongst other prized memorabilia from my reporting days. He thanked me for the story, described Peter's portrait as "the work of a Master Photographer" (hey, Joe was wonderfully photogenic!), and added: "May I say that while the Packet has such fine reporters and photographers, the Packet is bound to get better every year." He was a lovely, kind man and a delight to interview. I wish there were a few more like him to brighten our world.

Concrete Poetry: A Brief Liaison

1 Rejection Slip

```
P o e t r y
        t r y
        t r y
        t r y
        t r y
        t r y
        t r y
        t r y  a g a i n...
```

2 Liberty

```
liberty
liberty
liberty
liberty
liberty
liberty
liberty
liberty
liberty
liberty
 iberty
lib  ty
 berty
  ib
  er
  ty
```

Cormorant at Forty Paces

Solitary cormorant
Black as the island you guard
A solitary island
Licked by fitful waves
In ripple time.
You own this tiny crag of rock
You covet this barnacled sea bead
Even though it is minute,
Only about fifteen inches long
With a sweep of your muscular wings
And a wild shriek
Which scatters across the calm of the bay.
This is your land
Unless a kerosene invader
Captures more real estate
In its ugly wake.
A single, treadles tyre
Spins mournfully past
Through the grey-green waters
Like a cautious roundabout
At a rain-washed fair.
The cormorant ruffles its plumage
Are you blind as well as dumb, bird?
Your perch cannot resist invasion!
You peer at me
From under a dripping wing
No, not blind
Just a little dazed
By the world and its inconsistencies.
I think
I know
How you feel…

At Okehampton, February

The clouds are low today
And seem like misty mountain ridges
Capped with snow
Back-dropping a grey skyline.
Winter is passing.

A footprint cast in mud
Furrowed by tractor tyre ridges
Frozen in a final, fighting breath
Decries my cries for summer.

When will those sandy-surf months
Show face again?
They are so near
And yet so distant…

At the Mirror

On reflection
I think you are quite beautiful.
Yes, even as you comb-roam
Your sparkling golden hair,
Even as you mascara-squint
Your blues and greens and
Whoops! There goes the eyebrow tweezer!
Even as you squirt and spray
And pray that you look okay.
And the shimmer-glimmer
From a curtain-crack sun-body
Of utmost perfection
Makes my all-seeing eye gleam.
No, not too fat
No, honestly!
This dress or that dress
Well, if you want my opinion…
Oh, *that* one
Yes, well, if you must be
The Belle of the Ball.
Fabulous!
Makes me jealous
He really is a lucky guy.
I wish you were taking me with you
But the chest of drawers
Sort of pins me down…

75

I Mourn the Loss
Ruminations at 3am

I mourn the loss
>of all the girls I've ever loved
>of all the friends who sailed away
>and never kept in touch

I mourn the loss
>of family
>of uncles, aunts and cousins,
>dad and mum,
>the best and most of all
>of special pets - the cats, the dogs,
>the birds in cages and their songs

I mourn the loss
>of innocence and happiness
>of picnics, moments in the sands,
>of sunny summers,
>simple, loving times

I mourn the loss
>of places worked and people known
>of places seen and lost in time
>of silly trappings - cars and books,
>old toys and records, little things

I mourn the loss
>of youthful health
>I took for granted
>and simple joys
>I thought would last

I mourn the start
>of loneliness
>of separation, sadness, fear and isolation
>dissipation of my dreams
>and memories now a raw sciatic nerve

Then, once again
>it's all an illusion
>summoned to distress and pain
>I am just a part of all things
>whether they are now or elsewhere
>here for just a fleeting moment
>briefly as a butterfly
>Trying to make sense of living
>with a map that has no pointers
>aiming just to do my bit

The thought that came
>it is now fading
>cannot quite retain the vision
>There's a path and I am on it
>still have views to left and right
>still have views behind and forwards
>some more distant than at one time
>Always part of me for ever
>til I cease to need that ego
>Life does not revolve around me
>Things that leave are always present
>Now is always three locations:
>yesterday, today, tomorrow

So I mourn the pointless mourning
Til it goes, along with I.

Joy to be Alive
Reminiscences of three friends

For HN

Now winter creeps upon the grass
And ice glazes the pool
Where we would sit and watch the stars
On a summer's evening cool
The rooks would chatter into dusk
And gradually subside
And we would touch the morning
With the joy to be alive.

For PG

And in the steamy restaurant
With cigarettes alight
We'd talk for hours of songs
Into the comfort of the night
Recalling days that we have known
And where we have arrived
And we would greet the evening
With the joy to be alive.

For JH

The tarmac surface of the road
Became your playground wide
Past flashing cliffs and sandy beaches
Laughing, side by side
And though you could not name the trees
The woods became your skive
And touched your happy eyelids
With the joy to be alive.

81

Misconceptions

Child:
"Mummy, where do I come from?
Daddy says it was the milkman!
Did I come with the gold top?
Did I come with the cream?
Did I come with the yoghurt?
Can you answer my dream?
Was I riding in the front seat?
Was I wearing the milkman's cap?
Was I just behind his horse?
Oh, can you tell me that?
I wouldn't mind so much if I knew
But the milkman doesn't look at all like you."

Mother:
"Sonny, where did you come from?
Daddy may have said it was the milkman!
You have always been my gold top
You have always been my cream
You have always been my yoghurt
You have always been my dream
You have ridden in the front seat
For you're such a precious chap
You have filled my life with love
Oh, I can you tell you that
I wouldn't mind so much if I knew
But the milkman doesn't look at all like you."

Father:
"Oh, honey, where did he come from?
Jokingly, I said it was the milkman!
You have always been my lover
You have always been my life
You have always been my woman
Seems you've always been my wife
I was riding in the front seat
I was wearing a milkman's cap
I was just behind the horse
Yes, I can tell you that
I wouldn't mind so much if I knew
But the milkman is a little anxious too."

Moments of isolation

I
Two men
Passing one another
On a long and empty stretch
Of desert track.
The one he looks up,
The other he looks down;
And their world
Safely retains
Its endless desolation.

II
One leaf fell
And as it fell
It brushed a flower.
The flower
Shook its tiny head in sympathy
And the leaf
Continued falling.
Neither spoke.

III
It seems an Eternity
Since we last
Held each other's hands
Kissed, or smiled
Our silent understandings.

IV

White owl
Against the snow
Which of you
Will the sun
First set to flight?

V

Do not follow
Little lost dog
Little mongrel
Thin and shabby
In a dirty street
On your last legs
Desperate
You know your Master calls
And I am not He.

Night-folded

I turn, in anticipation
Between the sheets of my imagination
And feel your scented presence
In a night of long serenade.
Your long, naked limbs reflect the moonlight
And your silky hair explodes across the sheets.
Your eyes are wide, then closed, in unspoken histories
And chapters new of our story old.
I feel your hesitant breathing
Against my resting chest
And sense the pulse of your sighs.
The moon spills dewdrops of perspiration
Across your soft-slumber lips.
But, as I bend to kiss
Morning comes
And I awake
Clutching a crumpled pillow.

Wedding Day

Confetti spaghetti
curls upwards on the spiky breeze
in thoughtful spiral
from the empty stones.
Leaf and horseshoe
(of course, you saw them too),
bells and triangles:
paper butterflies
to guide you away.

And where was I?

Looking for something
lost in the dust
that time had carelessly
blown away....

To Be Home Again

I: Outside

He opened his eyes.
A watery yellow sun was rising
over the silver-ice surface
of the metallic landscape;
a thin, chill mist was spreading in
from the South.

The hard ground
Beneath his scattered limbs
glistened with the light
of many water droplets.
His breath scattered on the still air
in thin but smoky eruptions.

Over the whole visible landscape
there was sign of neither
bird nor beast
flower nor tree
only the inflexible expanse of steel.
Neither bolted nor welded
were the sections of the Below,
rather joined by some invisible amalgamation
suggesting some great Whole
rather than a series of incongruent parts.

95

Cold to the touch, its extremities
but deep inside the imposing shell
the motion of many engines could be felt.
What form these devices took
the visitor's confused mind could only guess.
He sat up abruptly, as if paged by an off-stage aside
and gazed about him.

The past was suddenly as nothing,
like the accepted appearance
of dawn and dusk each day
(in the real world),
the future only a word with empty echoes.
He long considered his thoughtless excursion
then stood, ran fingers through his damp hair.

Beneath heavy, troubled lids
his eyes were blue and kind,
his mouth small and calm,
his locks long, brown, lank
and ploughed with many curly furrows.

He took a step forward – and fell.
The ground moulded to accommodate his frame
like a great gelatine mould
then returned without murmur
to its solid state, unyielding once more.
The sun was now glowing a deep orange
reigniting the Below with new signs.
The Above was still swathed in mist
but further light was creeping through
from some as yet undetermined place.

He lay where he had fallen for some time
Nothing made any sense
The silence was oppressing
Not even the mist was whispering
There was just the progressing sensation
of those vibrating under-surface motors
to reach out and grasp:
the tangibility of something material.
If only there was some way, he thought,
of reaching those beautiful masters
of physical senses, hidden below.
For a moment he lost control,
Spread-eagled himself,
pounded fruitlessly on the surface.
But his strokes made no sound
and the glare of that façade, that shell
remained unchanged, soft, seductive.

The sun was glowing red
when he ventured to stand once more
and a barely discernible new light
was trickling in from the West.
It was not red, but its hue was unknown.
He decided it was time to walk.

II: Trek

His march was long and monotonous
and the horizon towards which he plodded
seemed to retreat at his every footfall.
All around him stretched the leaden terrain
of the Below.
Before him, the horizon,
behind and beside, the whirling mist.
Not even his own steps
broke the empty pall of silence.

For perhaps the length of a morning
he continued his trek,
his forehead beaded with sweat
soon whisked away or dried in situ
by the isolated clouds of cold mist
that commuted from South to North
across his uncertain path.
The stillness remained as deep and brooding;
the surface of the land did not change.

He was close to exhaustion
when he came upon a crater
some four metres across with similar width and depth.
At first it seemed a perfectly constructed
Concave, circular moulding.
Looking closer he saw the sides
were unsymmetrical and ragged
as if unworked or incomplete.
Could it be that some descending object
of great size and weight
had impacted this sterile electroplated surface?
An object in part defeating any surface resistance?
If so, where was this interloper now?

He was no scientist and could not be sure of anything.
He could not even be sure who or what he actually *was*.
He glanced at the Above, hastily, indecisively
and realised that this was the first time
He had looked up at what might have been a roof.
Or, at least, a somewhere-else,
a place other than this strange land beneath his feet.
Little could be seen.
The sky (if indeed it was a sky)
Was dark and cold and filled him with fear.

A great foreboding burrowed into his skin.
The mist eddies were curling away
and the advancing red light
painting new, deeper colours
around the borders of the secret ceiling:
there was nothing more, except for
a terrible feeling of nothingness.
Dizzy now, he looked back down.

The strange crater had disappeared.
For a moment he wept, openly, loudly,
with a profound yet unfathomable despair,
as if losing a loved one of many years association;
denied his one chance to escape
the empty, incalculable, swirling Hell around him.
Angrily he stamped on the ground below,
then, falling to his knees, he pounded his fists
mercilessly into the unyielding floor.

All at once there was a fiery hiss,
as of something drawing a deep breath,
and the indistinct sky appeared to spin like a demented top.
A flash of light, so pure and dazzling
that he had to shield his eyes with shaky hands,
burst from the West and bit into the land beneath him
with thunderclap intensity.
He was suddenly aware of a piercing blackness
An ear-splitting roar, a metallic howl,
And the surface broke in two –
a pause
a feeling of weightlessness –
and then closed behind him again as he fell.

III: Inside

He opened his eyes.
He ran his hands over his arms and legs
but he seemed unhurt.
All around him, lit with a pale light,
mighty iron machines stood, row on row,
their gleaming pistons rising and falling
with the crushing might of a fatal cataclysm.
Grey steam and oil spewed from fractures
in the monsters' sheer and towering sides
like infected rainclouds from a holocaust winter.
The new Above was black, impenetrable;
the floor shook with the crush of industrial torment.
There were no walls, just rows of machines,
disappearing into a carbon infinity,
crashing, spitting, hammering, screaming.

Slowly a smile crept across his tearstained cheeks
and the visitor struggled to his feet.
Arms outstretched, he tottered across the great hall,
this immense, harsh and thunderous factory,
this place of steel and heat and shuddering convulsions,
this inferno of incomprehensible purpose,
and he fell at the feet of the largest of all the paraphernalia,
rising many metres into the darkness of the new Above
and again he wept. But this time with joy.

109

"I know you!" he cried, though his words could not be heard
through the great clamour.
"I feel you!" he cried.
And though he would never hear again,
his eardrums shattered by the chaotic din,
he had found something he could understand
something that would stay with him,
something to calm him in its blast and clamour
and he would never be lonely again.
He slumped into a ball on the floor and slept.
And that sleep was the sleep of the contented.
It was like being home…

The Intruder

Co-ordinator

Once,
when the world was just a shriveled orange
spinning in the mists of its own creation
when the sand and the seas were no more than
glimpses through the mirror of the Second Stage
when time was all and nothing and Infinity
merely an extension of the Now
when all was open, and ready for thought
came the Decision.

Intruder:

Where, where, where-not?
When? Why? When-why? Who? WHO?

Love:
(*at first singing beautifully and wordlessly to herself,*
as if not aware of the fresh presence)

Intruder:

Where? When? Why? Who? WHO?

113

Love:

Words...
The feeling of something new
Where before there was only fire
fire so beautiful and generous
now there is a way,
a way to express the fire, to spread the fire,
to illuminate the Universe...

Intruder:

Who?

Love:

I am Love...
There is only love, love is
All else grows from love
Love never appears, never lives, never dies
It is
Love never sleeps, never wakes, never cries
It will be.

Intruder:

But love is not where love has never been.

115

Love:

There are oceans of change coming. I must travel beyond.

Intruder:

Where, where, where-not?
When? Why? When-why? Who? WHO?

Peace:

Love has taught me words and those words
have transformed the Now, redressed the Forever
there are greater patterns to build within the fire.

Intruder:

Who?

117

Peace:

I am Peace.
When love calls, peace embellishes her path
Where the wind sleeps
Where the mists creep
Where the land is not invaded
Where the leaf sings
Where the brook springs
Where the light has not faded
Peace will be near, guard it well
For Peace is the Love you have found.

Intruder:

But peace is not when love has not been.

Peace:

There is truth here, but misplaced. Leave now.

Intruder:

Where, where, where-not?
When? Why? When-why? Who? WHO?

119

Harmony:

I am Harmony.
Where love and peace are joined
there can only be harmony.

Intruder:

You are direct.

Harmony:

There is honesty in direction, stability in existence
I am because they are
and because they are as two and as one
I exist and cannot be changed
Where Love may fall to your words
Where Peace may surrender to her parallel's
unpredicted change in direction
for as long as Love and Peace stand together
between the borders of the tangible and the indefinite
Harmony will flower
For Harmony cannot be changed by whim or whimsy
Or by the discoloration of her elements
But only by the loss of one.

Intruder:

But harmony is not where love and peace have never been.

Co-ordinator:

And the three essential lights of the Universe paused, and asked
"Who is this Intruder?"
And the intruder said

Intruder:

I am Man.

Co-ordinator:

And suddenly there were many stars
flickering and glinting in the confusion of Forever
and the world that was but a shriveled orange
transformed,
green and blue
beautiful, enticing
occupied
And discord was born.

123

Season

Smile now friends and counter-friends
It's that season of the year
Colour your cheeks with a fire of friendship
Love and fun and cheer
Delight at the spinneys and arbours
And respect all that you fear
For you know that the time is right
In that season of the year.

Remember, My Son

Remember, my son
Always remember:
Today you met your mama
Does it hurt to cry?

Just where the sunbeam
Divided the trees
Lighting the bumpy ground
The way she gently coloured my life
Yes, there.
Where the roses blew to and fro
And simple words of Goodbye
Mark and remark of her magnificence
Alone?
Oh, so alone, my son!

From a crowd of fools
Who trampled her down
To a silent, solitary place
Cold and dark
Wrapped in wood
Just there.
But, son, lonelier still
Had we been blessed with time
And you had been born.
Does it hurt to die?

Remember, my son
Always remember
Today you met your mama
Does it hurt…?

When Rabbits Go Bad (feral version)

Trying to be something you're not…
This is the more solemn version of the humorous poem
in my equivalent comic verse/cartoon book When Rabbits Go Bad,
also available from Amazon

128

When Rabbits Go Bad (feral version)

It's terribly sad when rabbits go bad
They stalk through the underbrush beating up field mice,
Threatening badgers and chasing off rooks with clubs

They dress like freebooters with cutlass and pistol
Check shirts, red bandanas, black pants and thigh boots
They growl and they snarl just like dogs in a cage

These grassland buccaneers, floppy-eared plunderers
Whiskery privateers – deer-jacking, pet-napping,
Sacking a squirrel den, pelting them with their own nuts

Fluffy is Blackbeard and Floppy is Captain Kidd
Sharpening their carrot blades with cold-eyed wickedness
Pillage and plundering supplanting foraging

Making a costume from lettuce and mosses
Hollowed-out acorns for firearms and skulls
No time to eat, caught up in the escapade

Wanted a life of crime, wanted some self-import
Sick of the warren life, paltry and tedious
Fancied the Spanish Main down in the woody copse

Like to flip black beetles on to their tergum
Then watch them struggling in disorientation
Spin them a few times then leave them helpless

Swordfights with ferrets and weasels and stoats
Terse confrontations among the dry leaves
Once afraid of them, now chasing them off

After a week or so both rabbits flagging
Limp in their picaroon (discarded fruit bowl)
No strength remaining to be the corsair

It's terribly sad when rabbits go bad
Neglecting to nibble while looting and ravishing
Fluffy and Floppy both legs-up, expired

129

Stock Car Racing

a frowning grey plume of candyfloss cumulus
gravely mounts her trembling summergreen pine steed
as backcloth to a million dollar epic
one thousand eyes for cameras
the failing sun for light
close at hand, buzz saws from a timber yard
razing a sandy clearing in a crown of rocks, gnawing
Valhalla grove; epitaphs in tree trunks
Let sentinel amber dust cloud spark the senses
erect a monument to fell grief:
confiscated willow, the healthy sunshade
that became a wicker basket

from the muddy, circular track: a spitting roar
oakapple candelabra shudder
committees of velvet green whisper and snap
in the short breeze
a colleague stretched lazily on the ground
sucks a sliver of grass between white teeth and snickers
to some joke of his own
"You can get grass poisoning," someone says
he shrugs

131

then, with a joust-like chequered flash, the race is on!
fifteen muti-coloured metal dragons unwind
spring from their haunches, explode into action
ferret-nosing each other
wheel cracking wheel, speedsteam
man/mud: a unity of purpose

a miscalculation!
brakes scream, a sick crunch, dust
a mountain of twisted steel confronts
"Would the mechanics next to that pool of petrol"
loudspeaker drones
"please extinguish their cigarettes"
adds, with conviction,
"not, of course, by dropping them into it"
all laugh, no-one hurt
tension slackens, as from a first-acquaintance smile
or vigorous handshake
the race starts (fresh from the blocks) once more

a silhouetted aircraft drift-drones overhead
an occasional albatross seeking a perch
and the sun shyly slips away, it's day's work done

133

SPOTLIGHTS!
exploding into the dusk
my grass-chewing colleague leans back
to rest his head on his girlfriend's handbag
Wait a minute! I cry
There's an earwig on it!
He flicks a hand, and there is no longer insect invasion
I yawn
the noise, the smell of second-hand fuel, is not to my taste
begging for relief from guttural engines
and the crash and scream of tight, rubber-grinding circuits
I'm just there for the company

all at once, it stops
SILENCE
no jokes and no cars, is it over?
a minute pause, the space between shaken awake and awakening
a frightening rip in Time
amplified by dull thoughts
suddenly Curly laughs
shatters the emptiness
(a little late in seeing a joke)
and Life is restored
(she is my Lily of Lacuna...)
the preoccupied drone of harsh competition
re-emerges, as from a heatherdown fog,
and the crazy contest goes on, and on, and on...

I'm hungry!
Look, a chip van!
I'd like some!
Come on, then!
the closing stages of the pageant
and preparation for the velvetdrop of night,
curtaincall, sporadic cricketmatch applause
everyone is leaving
in a dash for the cars
a cedilla of hair glued to Curly's forehead
amplifies the lampmoth frenzy to escape NOW
before we get hemmed in
our grassblade orator offers dull facts on vehicles,
those twisted chariots lined up on the course,
smoking, exhausted, while drivers disrobe
and the air becomes noticeably cold
the chill of goodbyes, of "see you again" (we hope)
Ignition, lift off, GO

Where was my sweetcorn princess tonight?
if only she had materialised briefly,
smiling diamonds, wrapped in her décolleté striped dress
warming my heart, caressing my eyes
Ah, my foolish indulgence in pointless imaginings
must fade and bide its time
a danger of *furor poeticus*
the divine frenzy of poetic madness
more fatal than crashing old bangers together!

The Secret Audience

The laughing faces in the rain
The empty quiet as you find a place to stay
The shelter with the leaking drain
The soggy heat haze and the smell of Gabardine
He strokes the bubbles from her eyes
She takes the moment to evaporate a frown
You know that only Time will sigh
As you envelope in the snuggle of your love
And the secret audience is there…

The parkside bench with creaking planks
The doubled shoulders of the one who came to rest
He feeds the birds like other "cranks"
With crumbs and nuts crushed in a crinkled paper bag
He knows the "gentlemen" by name
They swoop and call as if they really understand
A mittened hand shows they are tame
A sudden movement and they scatter to the wind
And the secret audience is there…

The room is square, you are alone
The coughing candle shows the shadows how to dance
An emptiness you will condone
To cut yourself off from the clamour of the day
The secret audience is there
The walls have ears and eyes and smell and taste and speech
The unobtrusive intruder glare
Will one quick cut disperse the villains of the peace?
And the secret audience despairs…

Merely On Hornsey Mere

The ducks are standing guard
on the still surface of Hornsey Mere.
The sun is wearing its long golden neckerchief
and the marshalling reeds
are bound to their silhouettes in shadowy salute:
the irrefutable call of the wild
suddenly alive within an artist's dream.
His bold and brilliant brushstrokes
sweep a clarity through life's disorder
calming my bruised mind
and Time, for a moment, pauses –
stilled on canvas.

Old

To be old
In an impersonal world
Hand crooked
Holding that lifegiving cigarette
Second hand clutching cane
Though there is no need
Domed head in flat cap
Gazing with vague awareness
From steel wheelchair
Rug over lap
A push from a youth
In a brown nylon shirt
Who leans on the handles
For a moment
Pauses at a shop window
For you to reflect
On your former self
When the only wheels you needed
Were on your pushbike
A passer-by stops
Chatters with brown shirt
Just everyday nonsense
You listen
As you have no choice
But your eyes are far away
Looking back
To when you were young
With so much promise
A nod
A push
And you are gone.

143

Winter's Despair

Winter is the mountain of despair
When every wind sighs Farewell
Every eye hides a tear.

Winter is the season
When all the summer shops
Board their windows
Closing their reflective eyes
On the empty cobbled streets.

Winter is the ice age of our evolution
When grey and grumbly waves
Spit and crash in violent upheaval
Against the abandoned coastline.

Winter is the alter of night
On which the sun dies.
Spidery trees hide their finery
And slender stalks sleep
Under a woolly blanket of cruel snow.

The sky is bleak
And the colours of mid-summer faded,
Dying, or already deceased
And the loves of the Hay Time
Lie buried in a coverlet of shadows.

145

We huddle, in a muddle
Will we make it through these leaden days?
Maybe if we keep our hearts warm, eyes bright,
Our choices and our plans plain and pure
Our moods calm, our thoughts clear
Dreaming of the joy of that first warm day

That day when we can breathe a sigh
And feel the lightness in the air
The golden glow on fields and houses
And we can say with deep relief
Reprieve! It's over, for another year

147

III Resolution

Girl on a Swing

An old man on the brink of ending his life finds new hope in new life.

Hey, little girl on the silver swing
What heights can you explore
Riding on your pendulum express
Encompassing the world?
Have you listed to the summer
Change to autumn on a cloud
Can you help an old man
Make up his mind
Before the coming of the crowd?

Hey, little girl, let's float down to the pond
Feed the ducks and count the weeds
Please forsake your silver swing
And gather up your beads.
You can wonder at a flower explode
Sending parachutes away
You can help an old man
Make up his mind
On whether he should stay.

Little girl, your hair is soft and blows
In the breath of someone's dreams
You alone can bring me memories
Of days of innocence long seen
By the City you will soon be called
But your beauty will be free
You have helped an old man
Discover in his mind
Just who he's meant to be.

149

Strange Evening with a Good Book

Read me something
By the dying candlelight
Let me conjure up fields I would have known
And could have known
If I had not been sheltering in an imagined pillbox!

The rain slushes down beneath stylish planks
Into the concrete foundations of our folly
We should have brought a brolly
And stayed in the fresh remains of the rain
Away from this dark drain
Funneling away, it seems, the good and the few.

Read me something
As the fire allows its final sparks
To blink and splutter
Let me delay the rays of light!

Cramped loosely
In a flood of whirling lights
Your leg against mine
Moving like the wheat to the beat
Of a special juggernaut of sound
Rising and falling like swollen doves
To the endless rhythms
Interchanging, crossing, penetrating
Through the closeness of our thighs
In a bucket at a fairground
In the last second of forever
I thought of... nothing.

Read to me, please
Dispel the doubts
That what we are doing is right.

Candyfloss cumulous
The glow of your smile comforts the horizon
And the evening birdsong
And the lumbering dodgems' lights
Coast through the curls of your hair
Finding hot dogs in chequered tents
Finding silence in a kiss.

Another page, please, quickly
Before the watery strange dawn
Floods the flower-curtained windows
And sets the silent shadows to flight
Back into the crevices.

The emerald water undulates and gurgles
Like a happy baby at the feeding bottle
And the tiny boat becomes our escape
And our security
Ponytails of seaweed roll sleepily by
Stirring shoals of minute silver fish
Each scurrying in its own hasty direction.
You tip the black fun hat saucily
(Bought in a seaside market)
With the air of a carefree bandido
I trail a hand in the lukewarm water
And dream of Greece.

A new chapter
Stop the coals from dying, unremembered
Save the day from advancing
To a checkmate reflection
On the fireside lino.

We are going home
Where we have been seems not to matter
We are together
Wheels spinning into the future
And the sky, though dimming
Is still blue.
You cross your bare legs across my lap
And snuggle against the door handle
Can you be comfortable?
Can I still drive?
You show no signs of distress
You sigh
I changed gear without obstruction
Your legs move with the motions of the car
In languid abandon
You say nothing
No words required...

The book is ended?
How else shall I recall those precious moments?
The reader rises, to leave
I give my thanks, regretful at our parting
The door closes
I am alone.

The consuming silence is long and weighty
The fire is dead
From the window the first tinges of morning
Are crawling over the dried putty
I claw at my sanded eyes
Dawn…
A sudden lurch of light
As of someone turning up a gas lamp
Blinks into the room
And touches the closed book on the floor.

How else shall I recall
Those precious moments?

I cross to the dusky wardrobe mirror
And peer hopefully into that looking glass world
Of backwards furniture
The great reverse
Does this now make my book unread?
I laugh at my foolishness
For things undone there is no mending…

How else shall I recall?
How else?

And yet…
I need no collages of endless meaningless lines
To fill my eyes with pictures of yesterday
For yesterday is with me always
In the wind, in the rain
At sea, on land
Sleeping, waking.
Every bee-buzzed cornfield
Reminds me of the flailing delight of your unfettered hair
Every drop of water reminds me of the depths of your eyes
Every street reminds me of the places we have been
Every landscape reminds me of the hills and vales of your skin

I need not recall
You are always
With me.

.

Beneath a Pupil Sea

You
Have the kind of depth
I could sit around a log fire with
in the snuggliness of winter;
the sort of depth
that moves mountains
and replaces them
with trees.
Your depth
is not of this world,
nor of any One,
but of many.
Your depth
is not for coffee cup quadrilles,
not scullery skullduggery:
it is for an age
that we have not yet seen
and perhaps
never will.

Another Day, Another Life

You're always glad to see me
And the feeling that you're there means all the world to me.
There's something in your laughter
And just knowing that you're there takes all the pain from me.
You are something special, like a rose or an Alpine sky
You're the Lady of the Lake,
You're the province that the fake couldn't occupy
You're a summer without end, you're a lover,
You're a friend, you're a dream of life
You're a poet, you're a priestess, you're a writer,
You're an artist, you're a wife.
You're the one who made the one that wore the knife
Slip away, another day, another life.

You always take the high road
While the valley of the storm eats out its fearful sway.
You're eyes say It's a promise
And just knowing that you care enchants an endless day.
You're someone gentle, like a stream, or a windless night
You're a jewel in its case, you're the everlasting face
On a cloudy kite.
You're a winter without snow, or a snowstorm with a glow
A joyous playground time
You're an actor, you're a woman, you're a treasure,
You're a teaser, you're sublime
You're the one who made the one that tossed the dime
Slip away, another day, another time.

Riverside

A goblet of wind
A quiet sea
And you, across a silver table
In candlelight
An unbelieving smile
As you accept the ring
Like the summer melting
Of winter snows
And even if it is too small
Only your finger knows.

A Torch in the Face of the Stars

Thoughts on the impenetrable cosmos.

As we plan to move further into space and explore other worlds, we might be minded to leave our destructive egos behind.

A Torch in the Face of the Stars

Strange Meeting

I have just met myself
In Time
And I do not like
What I see.

Presence

Starship trooper
To Starship Captain:
I think I can feel
The Edge
Of Everything.

Meteor

A meteor
Is a harsh thought
In the mind
Of the Universe.

Mariners

The Galaxy spreads
Like a golden sponge
The coral reef
Of our fishless ocean.

167

Message

"Scuttle my star ship
For I have betrayed
My race, my generation
And raped a planet
With my germ."

Celestial Objects

I
Venus lifts her satin veil
To expose
Yet another.

II
Saturn sleeps
Behind her smoke ring
Puffing away at the problem
Of who will come
When
And what to do
Then.

III
Mars projects her arteries
To pulsing prominence
Knowing that she will bleed
Upon the touch
Of the first footfall

169

IV
Moon.
A pale face
Of stardust grey
Gazes through blue hazes
From her Tranquility.
Her bruise is less painful now
But the next wound is soon.
There is really
Only one course.
A pale face
Resigns itself
And prepares
For her brainstorm.

Inscription
Beware
He who walks
In the land of the stars
And forgets
That he is a guest
In another's domain.

Gaze

By the bridge of two rivers

By the river of two bridges

The sun never sets

And the gentle insistence

Of your eyes

Calms even the waters

Of tears from timeless zones

Unleashed…

173

Heading Home

The summer's come and gone
The rain is chopping up the footprints that we left
The candles flutter out
In the stormy wind that rattles the casement wall
You are gone, together with the sun
There's nothing else, for all the good has gone
I'd like to call you for a day
To see if your sky's as blue as mine is grey.
Heading home – not on an aeroplane
Heading home – not on the sea
The love and memories you let me live
Are irreplaceable, irreplaceable to me.

Dream for that precious second, do you see a hill?
Our shadows are upon it still
And a tree, where we sheltered from the heat
The slow parade of donkeys on that cobbled village street.
Is it wrong to remember all those times
When I was yours, you were yours, and you were mine?

The tears they flow like rain
There's nothing left to stop them now that love has died
The kitten licks its paws
It can't remember when it hid in linen drawers
You are gone, together with that dream
There's nothing else, my love has passed unseen
I'd like to hold you for a day
Discover what made you go, made you stay.
Heading home – not on an aeroplane
Heading home – not on the sea
The love and memories you let me live
Are irreplaceable, irreplaceable to me.

175

God Blinked...

God blinked
And during that infinitesimal moment
They dropped the Bomb
He shouldn't have closed His eyes
He should not have ignored
The fighting, the antipathy, the hatred
For even such a little moment
But He did
And the world was wiped clean
The trouble was
The artists perished too
So there was no-one to see
To appreciate, to evaluate
The exquisite crimson/gold Atom sunset
Except the One who blinked
And He
Merely rubbed his hands
On the lamp of Existence
And started again...

Touch

And when the light of words flickers
Call softly upon the silk of touch
For touch is as a single drop of rain
On the unruffled surface of a pool
The union of a dew-petal
With a bright morning grass-blade
The flutter of an eyelid
On the first drizzly breath of a storm
The simple setting
Of a flamed sun on a glassy sea
The melting of a tender glance
The unfurling of a strand of wispy hair
The damp adornments on a spring spider's web.
For touch is the solution to a question
And the background to a reverie
And touch speaks
Where no spoken language can venture
No eyes can meet
No philosophies can cheapen.
With my fingers to your face
With my cheek to your hair
With my hand to your hand
With my heart to your heart.

Petals

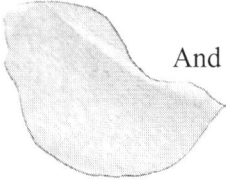

The first petal rose
And the freshness of a thousand dawns
Smiled into the sun.

The second petal rose
And a universal thought
Passed brightly through the galaxy.

The third petal rose
And the sky grew dark
And weeping willows
Shed tears of soot.

The fourth petal rose
And all the tears of lost generations
Served to wash the sleeping shores
Of Atlantis.

The fifth petal rose
And the sky was scorched with a yellow light
And consciousness became a volume
And not just a single page.

The sixth petal rose
And the arms of the cosmos
Reached out
And drank a faint memory.

181

IV Epilogue

on the shores of petemichael

It's hard to say goodbye, to weep the tears I need to shed
For you will always be with me and I will be with you
The songs we wrote, the laughs we had: one person now departed
A second person, eight years on: the fun, the happy journeys
Two friendships that will never end; you're both always nearby

So there's no need to say goodbye, you're in my mind forever
And in my heart, and in my soul, so fortunate to know you
So constantly I hear your voices, sense your presence in my world
And know that whilst I cannot see you, you're still here, at peace
Yet moved on to a better place, free from each-day trials and pains

So thank you both for all you gave, for all you shared and offered
You made my days much sunnier, much more fulfilled and special
I hear your voices all the time, that well-liked phrase or story
You're in my head, but quietly, emerging when the time's right
Instead, I'll just say "Hi" again; "hello" will follow later...

2020 Vision

2020 vision:
Normal visual acuity at twenty feet
Not perfect, of course
But a sign of how well you can see
Things like colour, moving objects
Different echelons of brightness.

Vision 2020: now perfectly flawed
Just enough to see the big E on the Snellen chart
Not enough to see the smaller signs
The ones whose murky shapes warn of danger:
Distorted images, even blindness.

2020: the Year of the Visor advisor
Hide your emotions in cloth and plastic
Never minded to call it drastic
We're all in it together, after all
Up to our necks.
"I can't breathe…"
Or think.

Under house arrest, under threat
Burned by the wicked fire of Fear
Of disinformation, cruel lies.
Crush those 'conspiracy theorists'
Before they are seen to be right.
Remember, with great power
Comes great irresponsibility.

185

Our precious country – our world – is dying
Not from a hyped-up virus
But a hyped-up autocracy.
No more than six together,
In or out
Split up families!
Don't trust that fresh air
Don't let your mask slip…
Are you all really
Happy to endorse this agitated lunacy?
As we follow the 'science'
That offers the most lucrative kick-backs.

Criticise our golden leader: guilty of sedition?
Inoculations to sidestep European Law
(Can't use the real V word!)
Unlicenced, poorly tested
Administered by non-medical replicas
Such as soldiers, midwives, physios
Perhaps a well-armed police officer?
A council handiman, willing street cleaner?
One of the new security thugs
Terrifying elderly people in supermarkets?
(Really? Anyone can jab you
With dangerous chemicals and it's OK?
So you'd take a flight with a blind pilot?)
And no legal recourse should you
Become sick (or die) from your treatment.

Emergency Powers (*Crisis, what crisis?*)
Testing scams: let's prove you have the disease
That needs the magic jab
(That's all of you, of course)
Not that you have active 'C'
(Can't use the condition's name either!)
As you are already immune!
Millions die, you say
But where are the streets and morgues
Stacked full of bodies?
God bless our suck-it-all-in Press.

2020: The dark days are truly here, after
Countless years of Austerity
Three years of Brexit denigrations
(Until "*Britannia Waives the Rules*")
Now a never-ending C-circus.
'Busybody Army' of ordinary citizens
Reporting their neighbours
Just in time for a Fourth Reich
While drugs chiefs with billions
Spread their inducements far and wide
From evasive politicians
To health principals
(With no principles)
To the humble small town surgery
(*Here's a nice payment each time*
You patient-ise these nice pills and jabs
To make the herd rattle and shake).

189

Where are our spiritual advisers
In this time of need?
Nodding along to the same geek chorus
And feeding from the same abundant high table.
Can't you be bothered to fight Evil anymore?
Are you quietly setting up new Ratlines
For the guilty to escape justice
If they ever receive the punishment they deserve?

An evergreen 2020:
Eighty years since the Battle of Britain
When brave young men
With hearts of oak
Saved us from tyranny
And died for their sacrifices.
Recall it well; wave flags.
But will no one be brave enough
To save us from tyranny now
In this new fascistic dawn?
For even the most beautiful landscape
Can be full of snakes.

"It will all be over by Christmas"
They hopefully said, six years before the end
Back in the days when there was still
More than just a sense of Honour.
On to a 2020 betrayal of those real heroes
With this cheating fiasco.
Eight decades away today
And your trusted medicos may be
More dangerous than the Luftwaffe.

"My glasses keep steaming up…"
Just a small dilemma.
Is it not the case that, for some,
Our *eyes and minds*
Have steamed up?

But there's still hope:
After all, a fool and the many
Are soon parted.
Time to awake…

If I could speak

If I could speak I'd tell you this
The world is strange and frightening
I was conceived before the Fear
And born at home in Lockdown
I could not see my parents' friends
Their friends, and their friends' children
I could not even go outside
For fear the air would kill me.
But there was one that was permitted
Not a relative or neighbour
She wore a white dress with a watch
Suspended from a pocket.
She wore a mask, so hard to hear
The words she told my mummy
But then I got a dreadful pain
A needle pushed into my skin.
Just two months in this crazy world
Yet much more sanctioned child abuse
To come.

If I could speak I'd tell you this
Don't fill me up with potions
If I could speak I'd tell you this
You're only going through the motions
Laid down by a careless state
That cares so little for my fate.
I'm new, I'm pure, I have no defects
Now you want an intervention
Like some selfish schoolroom prefects
Just in case I'm sick one day.
So came the needle's fine array
And as I squealed the nurse just laughed
"Oh, he'll get used to it!" she said.
"There's plenty more of these to come
And he'll be well protected."
A jolly cocktail for his health
We start with aluminium
With mercury, formaldehyde
Some beta-propiolactone
And monosodium glutamate
Pig blood, horse blood, rabbit brains,
DNA from humans too
From long-aborted babies...
Much like you, you little thing,
From one who didn't make it...

If I could speak I'd tell you this:
Don't give me jabs, don't give me creams
Just let my body screen itself
It's what it was designed to do.
But I can't stop you or say no
For while you act so unconcerned
And breeze your way so cheerily
There's something precious you've attacked;
Without the chance to make my choice
I cannot speak, I can't object
I can't stand up for tiny rights
All I can do's lie here
And scream…

In Britain most children have 21 jabs against 7 different diseases by their second birthday, starting at just 2 months old. In America young kids get more than 30 doses of 10 different jabs.